A Dictionary of Crick

Students Academy

www.draft2digital.com

# Copyright

Copyright@2023 Students' Academy

Published by: Education Corner

Draft2digital Edition

All Rights Reserved

Table of Contents

A
B
C
D
E
F
G
H
I
J
K
L
M
N
O
P

Q
R
S
T
U
V
W
X
Y
Z

## Preface

Welcome to "A Dictionary of Cricket Terms"! This comprehensive reference guide has been crafted by the passionate cricket enthusiasts at Students' Academy, who have dedicated countless hours to compile a treasure trove of cricket terminology for players, fans, and enthusiasts alike.

Cricket, often referred to as a gentleman's game, is a sport steeped in rich tradition, technical nuances, and a language all its own. From the thunderous sound of leather hitting willow to the strategic battles between bowlers and batsmen, cricket offers a captivating experience that extends beyond boundaries and transcends cultures.

This dictionary aims to unravel the intricacies of cricket terminology, serving as your trusted companion to navigate the vast array of terms encountered in the world of cricket. Whether you're a seasoned player seeking to refine your understanding or a novice fan eager to learn the game's lingo, this dictionary will be your go-to resource.

Within these pages, you will find an extensive collection of cricket terms meticulously organized in alphabetical order, enabling easy access to definitions, meanings, and insightful explanations. We have endeavored to capture the essence of each term, shedding light on their usage, historical context, and significance in the game.

In addition to providing clarity on commonly used terms such as "wicket," "boundary," and "googly," we have also included lesser-known gems like "silly mid-off," "yorker," and "zooter." Our aim is to offer a comprehensive understanding of cricket terminology, ensuring that no stone is left unturned.

It is worth mentioning that this dictionary is a collaborative effort of cricket enthusiasts, both young and old, who share a profound love for the game. We are indebted to the players, coaches, and cricket scholars who have contributed their knowledge and expertise, allowing us to present you with this invaluable resource.

We hope that "A Dictionary of Cricket Terms" will become an indispensable companion on your cricketing journey. May it enhance your enjoyment of the game, deepen your understanding of its intricate language, and foster a sense of camaraderie among cricket enthusiasts worldwide!

Wishing you hours of joy, enlightenment, and endless discoveries within these pages!

Sincerely,

Students' Academy

# Chapter 1

## A

### Abandon:

In cricket, abandon refers to the decision made to halt or cancel a match due to unfavorable playing conditions. This can be caused by factors such as inclement weather, which makes it impossible to continue the game, or if the playing surface is deemed unfit for play.

Example: The match was abandoned after relentless rain showers rendered the pitch waterlogged and unsafe for play.

### Aerial:

Aerial is a term used to describe a type of shot played by a batsman where the ball is struck high up in the air, often clearing the fielders and traveling a considerable distance.

Example: The batsman showcased his power and precision by executing a spectacular aerial shot, sending the ball soaring over the fielder's head and into the stands for a magnificent six.

**All-rounder:**

An all-rounder refers to a cricketer who possesses excellent skills in both batting and bowling, making significant contributions in both disciplines of the game. These players are known for their versatility and ability to make an impact with both the bat and the ball.

Example: Andrew Flintoff was a true all-rounder, known for his explosive batting and ability to take crucial wickets with his fast bowling. His all-round skills made him a valuable asset to the team in all formats of the game.

**Appeal:**

Appeal refers to a formal request made by the fielding team to the umpire, seeking a decision regarding the batsman's play. The fielding team usually makes an appeal when they believe the batsman is out, such as for caught behind, LBW, or a run-out. It is a way to seek confirmation or clarification from the umpire regarding a potential dismissal.

Example: The fielding team erupted in a passionate appeal, convinced that the ball had made contact with the edge of the bat before being caught by the wicketkeeper.

### Arm Ball:

An arm ball is a type of delivery bowled by a spinner or a fast bowler that does not spin or deviate significantly from the straight line. It often surprises the batsman who anticipates spin or movement but instead faces a delivery that goes straight on.

Example: The spinner deceived the batsman with a well-disguised arm ball that skidded straight on, beating the inside edge of the bat and hitting the stumps.

### Arm Guard:

An arm guard is a protective gear worn by a batsman on the non-striking arm. It is designed to provide protection against injuries caused by the ball, particularly from fast bowlers who generate high speeds.

Example: The fast bowler's bouncer struck the batsman's arm, but thanks to the arm guard, the impact was absorbed, minimizing any potential injury.

**Arm Speed:**

Arm speed refers to the velocity at which a bowler's arm moves during their bowling action. The speed of the arm plays a crucial role in determining the pace and variations of the deliveries bowled by the bowler.

Example: The fast bowler's remarkable arm speed allowed them to generate immense pace, consistently troubling the batsmen with their thunderous deliveries.

**Ashes:**

The Ashes is a term used to describe the Test cricket series played between England and Australia. The origin of this term can be traced back to a satirical obituary that appeared in an English newspaper. The obituary humorously declared the death of English cricket and mentioned that the ashes of the deceased cricket would be taken to Australia, where they would be cremated.

Example: The Ashes series is a highly anticipated contest between England and Australia, with a rich history of intense battles for cricket supremacy.

**Average:**

Average is a statistical measure used to assess a player's performance in batting or bowling. In batting, it is calculated by dividing the total number of runs scored by the number of times the player has been dismissed. Batting average indicates the average number of runs a player scores per dismissal. In bowling, average is calculated by dividing the total number of runs conceded by the number of wickets taken. Bowling average represents the average number of runs conceded per wicket.

Example: The cricketer maintained an impressive batting average of 55, showcasing their consistency and ability to score runs consistently.

**Away Swing:**
Away swing refers to the movement of a cricket ball in the air, away from the batsman, when delivered by a fast bowler. It is a type of swing bowling where the ball curves away

from the batsman, making it difficult to make proper contact.

Example: The fast bowler's skillful delivery produced substantial away swing, deceiving the batsman and resulting in an edge to the wicketkeeper.

## Chapter 2

## B

**Bail:**

Bail refers to one of the two small wooden pieces placed on top of the stumps in cricket. If a bail is dislodged by the ball or the wicketkeeper while the batsman is attempting a run or gets stumped, the batsman is considered out.

Example: The fast bowler's yorker uprooted the bail, resulting in the dismissal of the batsman.

**Ball:**

The ball is the essential object used in the game of cricket. It is typically a hard leather-covered sphere, often red or white, which is bowled by the bowler towards the batsman. The ball plays a vital role in the game, as the bowler aims to deceive the batsman and dismiss them, while the batsman tries to score runs off the ball.

Example: The bowler released a swinging delivery, and the batsman played it defensively with the straight bat.

**Batsman:**

A batsman is a player from the batting team who takes his turn to face the bowler and attempts to score runs. The batsman's primary objective is to strike the ball with the bat and score runs by running between the wickets or hitting boundaries.

Example: The experienced batsman showcased his impeccable technique, leaving the ball outside the off stump.

**Bat:**

The bat is the wooden equipment used by the batsman to strike the ball. It consists of a handle connected to a blade, which is usually made of willow. The batsman uses the bat to defend against the bowler's deliveries, as well as to score runs by hitting the ball into open spaces on the field.

Example: The batsman gripped the bat tightly and played a well-timed cut shot, sending the ball to the boundary.

**Boundary:**

The boundary refers to the perimeter of the playing area in cricket, which is typically marked by ropes or fences. When the batsman hits the ball and it crosses the boundary without touching the ground, it is awarded four runs. If the ball crosses the boundary after bouncing on the ground within the playing area, it is awarded six runs.

Example: The batsman lofted the ball over the fielder's head, and it sailed over the boundary for a four.

**Boundary Line:**

The boundary line is the marked line on the ground that indicates the boundary of the playing area. It serves as a visual reference for determining whether a shot played by the batsman results in runs.

Example: The fielder made a tremendous effort to dive and prevent the ball from crossing the boundary line.

**Bouncer:**

A bouncer is a type of delivery bowled by a fast bowler. It is aimed short and pitched to rise steeply towards the batsman's head or body. The intention behind a bouncer is to force the batsman into a defensive or evasive action, creating a challenging situation for them.

Example: The bowler surprised the batsman with a well-directed bouncer that had him ducking to avoid getting hit.

**Bowling:**

Bowling refers to the act of delivering the ball from the bowler's hand towards the batsman. The bowler uses various techniques and strategies to outsmart the batsman and dismiss them.

Example: The bowler demonstrated exceptional control and accuracy in his bowling, making it difficult for the batsman to score freely.

**Bowling Average:**

Bowling average is a statistical measure that indicates the average number of runs conceded by a bowler per wicket taken. It is calculated by dividing the total runs conceded by the number of wickets taken.

Example: The fast bowler finished the season with an impressive bowling average of 18, showcasing his effectiveness in taking wickets and restricting the opposition's scoring.

**Box:**

A box, also known as a protective cup, is worn by male players to guard the groin area from potential injuries. It is an essential safety gear for batsmen and wicketkeepers to protect themselves from fast-paced deliveries.

Example: The bowler's fiery delivery struck the batsman's box, but he remained unharmed due to the protective gear.

Chapter 3

C

**Calling:**

Calling refers to the communication between the batsmen to decide whether or not to attempt a run after the ball has been played. It involves verbal communication, gestures, or a combination of both to coordinate their movements on the field.

Example: The batsman made a quick call for a run, and his partner responded promptly, resulting in a successful run.

**Captain:**

The captain is the player who is appointed to lead the team. They are responsible for making strategic decisions, such as setting the field placements, making bowling changes, and providing guidance to the players on the field.

Example: The captain's calm and composed demeanor inspired the team, leading them to a remarkable comeback victory.

**Carry:**

Carry refers to the distance the ball travels in the air after being hit by the batsman. It signifies the power and timing of the shot played.

Example: The batsman's elegant cover drive had excellent carry as the ball sailed over the fielders' heads and reached the boundary.

### Catch:

A catch occurs when a fielder successfully catches the ball after it has been hit by the batsman without it bouncing on the ground. If a catch is taken cleanly, the batsman is declared out.

Example: The fielder positioned himself perfectly and took a stunning catch, resulting in the dismissal of the batsman.

### Catching Practice:

Catching practice is a training drill conducted by teams to enhance the fielders' catching skills. It involves practicing various types of catches, including high catches, low catches, diving catches, and catching under pressure.

Example: The team dedicated extra time to catching practice, focusing on improving their technique and consistency in taking catches.

**Chin Music:**

Chin music is a colloquial term used to describe a delivery bowled at or around the batsman's head. The intention behind chin music is to intimidate or unsettle the batsman and disrupt their rhythm.

Example: The fast bowler sent down a barrage of chin music to keep the batsman on edge and prevent them from settling into a comfortable batting rhythm.

### Clean Bowled:

Clean bowled is a dismissal in cricket where the ball hits the stumps directly and removes the bails without any intervention from the batsman or their equipment. It is considered one of the most satisfying ways to dismiss a batsman.

Example: The bowler's yorker was executed to perfection, resulting in the batsman being clean bowled and the stumps being disturbed.

### Close Fielders:

Close fielders are fielders positioned in close proximity to the batsman, usually in catching positions. They aim to create additional pressure on the batsman and increase the chances of taking catches.

Example: The captain strategically placed close fielders around the batsman, anticipating a potential catching opportunity and aiming to induce a false stroke.

### Cover Drive:

A classic batting shot played on the front foot, the cover drive is a graceful stroke where the batsman drives the ball along the ground towards the cover fielding position. It requires precise timing and technique.

Example: The batsman leaned into the shot and elegantly played a cover drive, piercing the field and collecting runs.

### Cover Point:

Cover point is a fielding position on the off-side, situated between point and extra cover. The fielder positioned at cover point aims to stop drives and cut shots played by the batsman.

Example: The batsman struck the ball fiercely, but the fielder at cover point quickly moved to his right and made a diving stop.

### Cow Corner:

Cow corner is an informal term used to refer to the region of the field between long-on and deep midwicket. It is often considered a scoring opportunity for batsmen looking to hit big shots.

Example: The batsman unleashed a powerful slog towards cow corner, clearing the boundary for a six.

### Cricinfo:

Cricinfo is a widely popular website that provides live scores, news, statistics, and other cricket-related information. It is a go-to platform for cricket enthusiasts to stay updated on matches and players.

Example: Fans around the world relied on Cricinfo to follow the live scores and detailed commentary of the match.

**Cross Seam:**

Cross seam refers to a delivery where the seam of the cricket ball is positioned perpendicular to the pitch. This positioning can lead to variations in bounce and movement off the surface, making it challenging for the batsman.

Example: The bowler decided to deliver a cross-seam ball, hoping to extract extra bounce and surprise the batsman.

**Crease:**

The crease refers to the marked lines on the pitch where the batsman takes his position to receive the ball. It consists of the popping crease, which is the line closest to the stumps and determines the legitimacy of a bowled delivery, and the batting crease, which marks the back foot placement of the batsman.

Example: The batsman took a step forward, ensuring his front foot landed behind the crease to avoid a potential stumping.

**Cover Fielder:**

A fielder positioned on the off-side, typically between point and mid-off, is known as the cover fielder. This fielding position aims to stop drives and cut shots played by the batsman.

Example: The batsman struck the ball towards the covers, but the agile cover fielder quickly moved to his left and made a diving stop.

**Cricket Ball:**

The cricket ball is a hard, leather-covered sphere used in the game. It is traditionally red in color for Test matches and white in limited-overs formats. The ball's construction and condition significantly impact its movement and behavior during gameplay.

Example: The fast bowler delivered a swinging yorker, and the cricket ball crashed into the stumps, resulting in a wicket.

### Crease Occupation:

Crease occupation refers to a batsman's ability to stay at the crease for a considerable period without getting dismissed. It involves displaying strong defensive skills, shot selection, and patience, ultimately contributing to building a substantial innings.

Example: The batsman showcased remarkable crease occupation, frustrating the bowlers with his impeccable technique and disciplined approach to batting.

### Cricket Ground:

The cricket ground refers to the playing area where the game of cricket is contested. It encompasses the pitch, which is the central strip of carefully prepared turf, the outfield, which surrounds the pitch, and the various fielding positions where players are strategically placed.

Example: The cricket ground was bathed in sunshine as the teams took to the field for an intense battle.

### Cricket Whites:

Cricket whites are the traditional attire worn by cricketers during matches. They typically consist of white trousers and a white shirt, often accompanied by a cap or a hat.

Example: The players looked elegant in their crisp white uniforms as they represented their respective teams on the field.

### Cross-Batted Shot:

A cross-batted shot is a batting stroke where the batsman swings the bat horizontally across the line of the ball. This includes shots like the pull, hook, and sweep, which are executed by bringing the bat across the body.

Example: The batsman unleashed a powerful cross-batted shot, sending the ball soaring over the boundary for six runs.

### Cross-Seam Bowling:

Cross-seam bowling is a technique employed by bowlers where they position the seam of the ball perpendicular to the pitch. This alteration in the ball's orientation can lead to variations in bounce, making it difficult for batsmen to anticipate the delivery.

Example: The fast bowler opted for cross-seam bowling to exploit the uneven nature of the pitch and generate extra movement off the surface.

## Cumulative Average:

The cumulative average refers to the average score per innings, considering the total runs scored and the number of dismissals encountered by a batsman over a period of time or a specific series.

Example: The batsman maintained a high cumulative average of 55, indicating consistent performance throughout the season.

## Cut Off:

The cut off refers to the fielder's action of intercepting a throw from the outfield and preventing the batsmen from scoring additional runs. It involves quickly getting in the path of the throw and relaying the ball to the appropriate fielder or wicketkeeper.

Example: The fielder showed great agility and anticipation as he made a sharp cut off, preventing the batsmen from taking an extra run.

**Cut Shot:**

A cut shot is a batting stroke played by the batsman to hit the ball square of the wicket on the off-side. It involves using the horizontal bat to guide the ball behind point or cover.

Example: The batsman exhibited perfect timing and placement as he played a magnificent cut shot, sending the ball racing to the boundary.

**Cutters:**

Cutters are a type of delivery bowled by seamers where they grip the ball differently to generate cut and deviation off the pitch. The bowler alters the seam position or uses their fingers to impart spin or change the trajectory of the ball.

Example: The bowler showcased his mastery of cutters, deceiving the batsman with subtle variations in line and length.

Chapter 4

D

**Damp Pitch:**

A damp pitch refers to a cricket pitch that has absorbed moisture, usually due to rain or excessive watering. This can result in slower ball speed and lower bounce, making it more challenging for the batsmen.

Example: The bowlers exploited the conditions on the damp pitch, extracting movement and causing difficulties for the batsmen.

**Dead Ball:**

A dead ball is a situation in cricket where play is temporarily halted, and no runs can be scored or wickets can be taken. It is typically called by the umpire due to various reasons, such as the ball becoming unfit for play or an interruption in the game.

Example: The umpire signaled a dead ball when the bowler slipped during his delivery stride.

**Declaration:**

A declaration is a strategic decision made by the captain of a batting team to end their innings voluntarily, even if not all their batsmen have been dismissed. This is often done to set a target for the opposing team, allowing the game to progress.

Example: The captain made a bold declaration, setting a challenging target of 350 runs for the opposition to chase.

**Delivery:**

A delivery refers to the action of a bowler releasing the ball towards the batsman. It encompasses the entire process, including the run-up, bowling action, and the release of the ball.

Example: The bowler's smooth delivery resulted in a perfect yorker that crashed into the batsman's stumps.

**Direct Hit:**

A direct hit refers to a fielder throwing the ball accurately and hitting the stumps directly without any deflection, leading to a run-out. It requires precision and quick reflexes from the fielder.

Example: The fielder's direct hit from the deep caught the batsman unaware, resulting in a spectacular run-out.

### Disciplinary Action:

Disciplinary action refers to punitive measures taken against players who have violated the code of conduct or displayed unsporting behavior. These actions are taken to maintain the integrity and spirit of the game.

Example: The player was fined and suspended as a result of his disciplinary action for excessive appealing and using offensive language.

### Doosra:

The doosra is a delivery bowled by off-spinners, primarily in cricket, where the ball spins away from the right-handed batsman (for a right-arm off-spinner). It is a deceptive variation that challenges the batsman's ability to read the spin.

Example: The off-spinner bowled a perfectly disguised doosra, fooling the batsman into playing the wrong line and getting him stumped.

**Dot Ball:**

A dot ball refers to a delivery bowled by the bowler where the batsman fails to score any runs. The ball is played but does not result in the batsman getting off strike.

Example: The bowler maintained a tight line and length, forcing the batsman to play defensively, resulting in several dot balls in a row.

**Double Century:**

Double Century refers to an impressive feat achieved by a batsman in cricket when they score 200 or more runs in a single innings. It is a remarkable milestone that showcases exceptional skill, endurance, and concentration on the part of the batsman. Scoring a double century is considered a significant accomplishment in the game, often putting the batsman in the spotlight and contributing significantly to their team's total score. It is a testament to the batsman's ability to dominate the opposition's bowling attack and play a long, impactful innings. Double centuries are celebrated as remarkable individual achievements and are often remembered as memorable performances in the history of the sport.

Example: The opening batsman showcased a brilliant performance, scoring a double century with an array of boundaries.

### DRS (Decision Review System):

The Decision Review System (DRS) is an advanced technological system utilized in cricket to review and potentially overturn umpiring decisions. It enables players to challenge on-field decisions by requesting a review of the decision. The system incorporates several tools, including ball-tracking technology and hotspot cameras, to assist in the review process and detect any errors in the initial decision. This technology-based system has been instrumental in enhancing the accuracy and fairness of umpiring decisions in the game of cricket.

Example: The batsman was given out caught behind, but he was confident that he hadn't touched the ball. He decided to use the DRS to challenge the decision.

### Duck:

In cricket, a duck refers to the situation where a batsman gets dismissed without scoring any runs in an innings. It is often considered an unfortunate and disappointing outcome for the batsman.

Example: The experienced batsman was dismissed for a duck, caught at slip in the first over of the match.

### Duckworth-Lewis Method:

The Duckworth-Lewis Method is a mathematical formula used to calculate target scores in rain-affected limited-overs matches. It takes into account the number of overs lost due to rain and adjusts the target score for the team batting second accordingly.

Example: Heavy rain interrupted the match, reducing it to a 30-over contest. The target score for the chasing team was determined using the Duckworth-Lewis Method.

**Durham ball:**

A "Durham ball" refers to a delivery in cricket that exhibits significant swing, often occurring when the ball has become discolored or is older.

Example: The bowler executed a remarkable delivery known as a "Durham ball," which featured a late and pronounced swing. This unexpected movement left the batsman perplexed and struggling to respond.

Chapter 5

E

**Edge:**

When the cricket ball grazes the edge of the bat before being caught by the wicketkeeper or fielders, resulting in the dismissal of the batsman.

Example: The batsman's attempted shot resulted in a slight edge, and the wicketkeeper made a clean catch.

**Extra:**

Additional runs awarded to the batting team due to errors or penalties committed by the fielding team, such as no balls, wides, and byes.

Example: The bowler's delivery was wide, and the batting team was awarded an extra run.

**Economy Rate:**

The economy rate in cricket refers to the average number of runs conceded by a bowler for each over they have bowled. It is calculated by dividing the total runs conceded by the number of overs bowled. The economy rate is used as a measure of a bowler's effectiveness in restricting the opposition's scoring. A lower economy rate indicates that the bowler has been successful in conceding fewer runs, while a higher economy rate suggests that the bowler has been more expensive in terms of runs conceded. The economy rate is an important statistic used to assess a bowler's performance and contribution to the team's overall bowling effort.

Example: The bowler maintained an impressive economy rate of 4.5 runs per over throughout the match.

**Elbow Guard:**

Protective gear worn by a batsman on the front forearm and elbow to provide protection against impact from the ball.

Example: The batsman wore an elbow guard to safeguard against potential injuries while facing fast bowlers.

**Extras:**

Additional runs awarded to the batting team due to errors or penalties committed by the fielding team, such as no balls, wides, and byes.

Example: The team's total received a significant contribution from 20 extras, including 12 wides and 4 no balls.

### Scanning the Field:

The act of a batsman carefully observing and analyzing the field placements and positions of fielders before and during the delivery to make strategic shot selections.

Example: The batsman scanned the field, assessing the placement of the fielders and identifying scoring opportunities for his shots.

# Chapter 6

## F

**Face:**

The surface of the cricket bat that the batsman uses to strike the ball.

Example: The batsman played the ball with a straight bat, making contact with the middle of the face.

**Fast Bowler:**

A type of bowler who delivers the ball at high speed, aiming to generate bounce and pace off the pitch.

Example: The team relied on their fast bowlers to take early wickets with their raw pace.

**Fielder:**

A player positioned on the fielding team responsible for stopping the ball, catching, and fielding to prevent runs.

Example: The fielder at mid-off took a brilliant diving catch to dismiss the batsman.

**Fielding:**

The collective effort of the fielding team to prevent the batting team from scoring runs and taking wickets.

Example: The team's fielding was exceptional, with agile fielders saving numerous runs on the boundary.

### Fine Leg:

A fielding position on the leg side, slightly behind the batsman, towards the boundary.

Example: The ball deflected off the batsman's pads and ran away to fine leg for a boundary.

### First-class Cricket:

The highest level of domestic cricket, typically played over several days with longer match durations.

Example: The young cricketer made his debut in first-class cricket and impressed with a century.

### Flick:

A batting shot played by quickly turning the wrists to direct the ball towards the leg side.

Example: The batsman flicked the ball off his pads and picked up two runs towards mid-wicket.

**Follow-on:**

A situation in Test cricket where the team batting second is made to bat again immediately after being dismissed in their first innings, as the team batting first has a substantial lead.

Example: The team had a massive lead of 300 runs and decided to enforce the follow-on.

**Four:**

A scoring shot where the ball crosses the boundary after hitting the ground.

Example: The batsman played a glorious cover drive, and the ball raced away to the boundary for four runs.

**Full Pitch:**

A delivery bowled by the bowler that pitches on or near the popping crease, allowing the batsman to play aggressive shots.

Example: The bowler overpitched, and the batsman drove the ball down the ground for a boundary.

**Full Swing:**

A type of batting shot where the batsman swings the bat with full force in an attempt to hit the ball aggressively.

Example: The batsman executed a full swing and dispatched the ball over the mid-wicket boundary for a six.

## Chapter 7

## G

**Gallop:**
A quick run taken by the batsmen to score runs between the wickets.

Example: The batsmen completed a quick gallop between the wickets to take a single.

**Game of Cricket:**
The sport of cricket, played between two teams, involving batting, bowling, and fielding.

Example: The game of cricket requires skill, strategy, and teamwork to succeed.

### Gentleman's Game:

A term often used to refer to cricket, emphasizing its traditions, sportsmanship, and fair play.

Example: Cricket is known as the gentleman's game, with players adhering to the principles of fair play and respect.

### Gully:

A fielding position on the off side, close to the batsman, between the slips and point.

Example: The fielder positioned at gully took a sharp catch to dismiss the batsman.

### Googly:

A type of delivery bowled by a leg-spinner that appears to be spinning in one direction but actually spins in the opposite direction.

Example: The leg-spinner bowled a deceptive googly that spun away from the batsman and took his edge.

### Grip:
The way a batsman holds the cricket bat while playing shots.

Example: The batsman adjusted his grip to have better control over his shots against the swinging ball.

### Ground:
The playing area where the cricket match takes place, typically consisting of a pitch, outfield, and boundary.

Example: The cricket ground was well-maintained, providing a conducive playing surface for the match.

### Guard:

The position taken by a batsman to stand in front of the stumps while facing the bowler.

Example: The batsman took his guard before facing the next delivery, marking his preferred position.

### Gun Barrel Straight:

A term used to describe a delivery that is bowled in a perfectly straight line without any deviation.

Example: The fast bowler's delivery was gun barrel straight, beating the batsman's defenses and hitting the stumps.

Chapter 8

H

**Half-Century:**
A batting milestone achieved when a batsman scores 50 runs in an innings.

Example: The batsman completed his half-century with a boundary through the covers.

**Handled the Ball:**
A mode of dismissal where a batsman is given out if they intentionally touch the ball with their hand, without the permission of the fielding side.

Example: The batsman was given out for handling the ball when he tried to stop it with his hand.

### Hat-Trick:

When a bowler takes three wickets off consecutive deliveries in a single over.

Example: The bowler achieved a hat-trick by dismissing the batsmen with three successive balls.

### Hit-Wicket:

A mode of dismissal where a batsman is given out if they disturb the stumps with their bat, body, or equipment while playing a shot.

Example: The batsman was dismissed hit-wicket after his back foot hit the stumps while attempting a pull shot.

### Hook Shot:

A batting shot played by pulling a short-pitched delivery from outside the off stump towards the leg side.

Example: The batsman executed a powerful hook shot, sending the ball soaring over the square leg boundary for six runs.

### Howzat:

A traditional appeal made by the fielding team to the umpire, asking whether the batsman is out.

Example: The bowler and fielders shouted in unison, "Howzat!" to appeal for a caught-behind dismissal.

### Hundred:

A batting milestone achieved when a batsman scores 100 runs in an innings.

Example: The captain played a brilliant innings, reaching his hundred with a lofted shot for six.

Chapter 9

I

**Infield:**
The central area of the cricket field, closer to the pitch, where most of the fielders are positioned.

Example: The batsmen had to be quick between the wickets to avoid getting run out in the infield.

**Infielder:**
A fielder positioned in the infield, responsible for fielding the ball and attempting run-outs.

Example: The team had exceptional infielders who saved numerous runs with their agile fielding skills.

### Inning:

The batting turn of a team during a cricket match, comprising of one or two sessions.

Example: The team scored a massive total of 500 runs in their first inning.

### Inside Edge:

When the ball makes contact with the inside edge of the bat before going to the field.

Example: The batsman was fortunate as the inside edge prevented the ball from hitting the stumps.

### Insufficient Fielding:

A penalty awarded to the batting team when the fielding side fails to maintain the required number of fielders on the field.

Example: The batting team was awarded five runs for insufficient fielding due to a missing fielder.

### International Cricket:

The highest level of cricket played between national teams, representing their respective countries.

Example: The cricketer dreamt of playing international cricket and representing his country at the highest level.

### Intentional No-Ball:

A type of no-ball deliberately bowled by the bowler, often to restrict the scoring opportunities for the batsman.

Example: The bowler intentionally bowled a no-ball to prevent the batsman from freely hitting a boundary.

**Interference:**

A violation that occurs when a player obstructs or interferes with another player's ability to play a shot or field the ball.

Example:

The fielder was given a warning for interference as he obstructed the batsman's path while attempting a run.

**Inswinger:**

A delivery bowled by a fast bowler that moves towards the batsman in the air, curving inwards.

Example: The bowler generated swing and bowled an inswinger that beat the batsman's defenses.

## Chapter 10

## J

### Jack:

A slang term for a good batsman who is skillful and reliable.

Example: The team's star player was a jack with his ability to consistently score big runs.

### Jaffa:

A term used to describe an exceptionally well-delivered ball that is difficult for the batsman to play.

Example: The bowler bowled a jaffa that pitched on off-stump and moved away sharply, beating the batsman's edge.

**Jammy:**

A slang term for a batsman who manages to survive and score runs despite being in difficult or challenging situations.

Example: The batsman had a jammy innings, surviving several close calls and playing some streaky shots.

**Jolted:**

When a batting team loses quick wickets in succession, causing a sudden setback or disruption to their innings.

Example: The team was jolted early on, losing three wickets in the first few overs of the match.

### Junior Cricket:
Cricket played at the youth level, typically involving players below a certain age or experience threshold.

Example: The young cricketer honed his skills playing junior cricket before progressing to senior levels.

### Jumper:
A sweater or pullover worn by cricketers, usually made of wool, to keep warm during matches or practice sessions.

Example: The bowler wore a thick jumper to keep himself comfortable during the chilly morning session.

### Jury Stumps:

Stumps used during practice or training sessions, usually made of cheaper materials than official match stumps.

Example: The players used jury stumps for their net sessions to simulate match conditions.

### Juggling Catch:

A catch where the fielder initially fails to hold onto the ball but manages to regain control before it hits the ground.

Example: The fielder took a juggling catch near the boundary rope, delighting the crowd with his acrobatics.

**Jumping the Gun:**

When a fielding team prematurely celebrates a wicket before the decision is made by the umpire or technology.

Example: The fielders were guilty of jumping the gun, celebrating a catch that was later deemed not out after review.

Chapter 11

K

**Keeper:**

Short for wicket-keeper, the player who stands behind the stumps and is responsible for catching the ball and attempting run-outs.

Example: The wicket-keeper took a brilliant diving catch to dismiss the batsman.

**Knock:**

Refers to a batsman's innings or the act of scoring runs.

Example: The batsman played a fantastic knock, scoring a century in challenging conditions.

### Knocking in:

The process of preparing a new cricket bat by striking it repeatedly to compress the wood fibers and improve its performance.

Example: The cricketer spent hours knocking in his new bat before using it in a match.

### Knockout:

A type of limited-overs cricket tournament where teams compete in a single-elimination format, with losing teams being eliminated.

Example: The team reached the semi-finals of the knockout tournament but was knocked out by a strong opponent.

### Knuckleball:

A slower delivery bowled by a spinner or medium pacer, where the ball is released with the knuckles instead of the fingertips, causing it to skid and deceive the batsman.

Example: The spinner bowled a knuckleball that completely fooled the batsman, resulting in a clean bowled.

### Knocks:

Refers to the number of runs scored by a batsman in an innings.

Example: The opener scored quick runs and reached his fifty in just 35 knocks.

**Kookaburra:**

A brand of cricket ball commonly used in international matches and many domestic leagues.

Example: The bowler was delighted with the swing he generated with the new Kookaburra ball.

**Kwik Cricket:**

A modified version of cricket played with a soft ball and plastic equipment, often used for introductory or youth cricket.

Example: The school organized a Kwik Cricket tournament to introduce young children to the game.

## Chapter 12

## L

**LBW (Leg Before Wicket):**

A mode of dismissal in which the batsman's leg obstructs the ball from hitting the stumps, as judged by the umpire.

Example: The bowler appealed for an LBW, and after reviewing the replay, the umpire raised the finger.

**Late Cut:**

A batting shot played by guiding the ball behind the wicketkeeper towards the third man region.

Example: The batsman expertly played a late cut, finding the gap between the slip fielders for a boundary.

**Leave:**

When a batsman chooses not to play at a delivery and allows it to pass through to the wicketkeeper without attempting a shot.

Example: The batsman decided to leave the ball outside off stump, judging that it was going wide.

**Length:**

Refers to the spot where a delivery pitches on the cricket pitch, often categorized as full length, good length, or short length.

Example: The bowler consistently maintained a good length, making it difficult for the batsmen to score freely.

### Liberty:

The freedom given to a batsman to play shots without restriction, usually associated with a batsman in good form.

Example: The aggressive opener was given the liberty to attack the bowlers right from the start of the innings.

### Line:

The direction in which a delivery is bowled, typically categorized as outside off, on middle, or on leg.

Example: The bowler bowled a tight line just outside off stump, making it challenging for the batsman to score.

**Loopy:**

Describes a slow and high-arcing delivery bowled by a spinner, intended to lure the batsman into making a mistake.

Example: The spinner tossed up a loopy delivery, tempting the batsman to go for the big shot.

**Long Off:**

A fielding position on the off side, usually placed deep and slightly wide of the straight boundary.

Example: The fielder stationed at long off made a diving save near the boundary, preventing a certain four.

**Long On:**

A fielding position on the on side, usually placed deep and slightly wide of the straight boundary.

Example: The batsman lofted the ball over the bowler's head, but the fielder at long on took a comfortable catch.

Chapter 13

M

**Maiden:**

An over in which no runs are scored off the bowler, and no extras are conceded.

Example: The bowler bowled a maiden over, keeping the batsmen under pressure.

**Match:**

A single game or contest between two cricket teams.

Example: The team won the match convincingly, chasing down the target with overs to spare.

**Middle order:**

The batting positions in a team's lineup that come after the top order but before the lower order.

Example: The middle-order batsmen played crucial innings, stabilizing the team's total after early wickets.

**Mid-off:**

A fielding position on the off side, generally positioned between the bowler and mid-on.

Example: The batsman drove the ball straight, and the fielder at mid-off made a diving save.

**Mid-on:**

A fielding position on the on side, usually positioned between the bowler and midwicket.

Example: The batsman flicked the ball off his pads, and the fielder at mid-on collected it cleanly.

### Midwicket:

A fielding position on the on side, generally located between mid-on and square leg.

Example: The batsman played a powerful shot through midwicket, earning four runs.

### Mankad:

A controversial method of dismissal where the bowler, before delivering the ball, runs out the non-striking batsman if they leave the crease early.

Example: The bowler warned the non-striker for backing up too far and eventually mankaded him.

### Match referee:

An official appointed to ensure that the cricket match is played within the rules and regulations set by the governing body.

Example: The match referee penalized the team for their unsportsmanlike conduct during the match.

### Misfield:

A fielding error or mistake that allows the batsman to score additional runs.

Example: The fielder misfielded the ball, giving the batsman an opportunity to take a quick single.

Chapter 14

N

**Nap:**
The pile of fabric on the surface of a cricket ball caused by wear and tear during the game.

Example: The bowler noticed that the ball had a significant nap, making it difficult to grip and swing.

**Nervous nineties:**
Refers to the period when a batsman's score is in the 90s, often considered a challenging phase as the batsman approaches a century.

Example: The batsman was in the nervous nineties, feeling the pressure to reach his hundred.

**Nightwatchman:**

A lower-order batsman sent in to bat near the end of a day's play to protect a recognized batsman from facing the new ball.

Example: The team sent in a nightwatchman to bat for the last few overs of the day and protect the specialist batsman.

**No ball:**

An illegal delivery where the bowler oversteps the front line, resulting in an extra run for the batting team and a free hit for the batsman.

Example: The umpire called a no ball as the bowler's foot was clearly beyond the popping crease.

### Non-striker:

The batsman who stands at the opposite end of the pitch from the bowler, awaiting their turn to face the ball.

Example:

The non-striker was alert and ready to run whenever the batsman called for a quick single.

### Not out:

The decision given by the umpire when a batsman is not dismissed and remains at the crease.

Example: The fielding team appealed for a catch, but the umpire declared the batsman not out as there was no conclusive evidence.

**Nut:**

Slang term for the cricket ball.

Example: The fast bowler delivered a thunderous nut that swung away from the batsman.

**Number 11:**

The batsman who occupies the 11th and final position in the batting order.

Example: The number 11 batsman surprised everyone with some unexpected big hits, contributing valuable runs to the team's total.

Chapter 15

O

**Off drive:**

A cricket shot played by a batsman by driving the ball towards the off side, typically along the ground.

Example: The batsman played a beautiful off drive, timing the ball perfectly through the covers for a boundary.

**Off break:**

A type of spin delivery bowled by a right-handed off-spinner that turns from the off side to the leg side for a right-handed batsman.

Example: The off-spinner bowled an off break that spun sharply, beating the outside edge of the bat.

**Off side:**

The half of the cricket field that is to the right of a right-handed batsman or to the left of a left-handed batsman when facing the bowler.

Example: The batsman played a square cut shot to the off side, sending the ball racing to the boundary.

**On drive:**

A cricket shot played by a batsman by driving the ball towards the on side, typically along the ground.

Example: The batsman elegantly played the on drive, directing the ball between mid-on and midwicket for three runs.

**On side:**

The half of the cricket field that is to the left of a right-handed batsman or to the right of a left-handed batsman when facing the bowler.

Example: The batsman flicked the ball to the on side, finding the gap and picking up a couple of runs.

**One-day cricket:**

A format of cricket where each team gets to bat and field for a single day, typically limited to a specific number of overs per innings.

Example: The match was scheduled as a one-day cricket game, with each team aiming to score the most runs within their allocated overs.

**Opening batsman:**

The batsman who takes the crease and faces the first ball of an innings.

Example: The opening batsman played a crucial role in setting a solid foundation for the team's innings.

**Out:**

The dismissal of a batsman by the fielding team, resulting in the end of their batting innings.

Example: The batsman edged the ball to the wicketkeeper, and he was given out caught behind.

### Outfield:
The grassed area of the cricket field outside the pitch and square, where the ball rolls after being hit.

Example: The batsman hit the ball towards the outfield, and it raced to the boundary for four runs.

### Over:
In cricket, an over refers to a set of six legal deliveries bowled by a single bowler from one end of the pitch to the batsman at the other end. The bowler completes their action and delivers the ball six times consecutively, aiming to dismiss the batsman

or restrict the scoring. At the end of an over, the other end of the pitch is usually taken by a different bowler for the next over. The number of overs bowled by a team determines the progress of the game and helps track the number of deliveries remaining.

Example: The bowler bowled a tight over, conceding only three runs and taking a wicket.

**Overthrow:**

Additional runs scored by the batting team due to an errant throw by a fielder that goes past the stumps.

Example: The fielder's throw was inaccurate, resulting in an overthrow and an extra run for the batting team.

## Chapter 16

## P

**Pad:**

Protective equipment worn by a batsman on the legs to protect against being hit by the ball.

Example: The batsman played a defensive shot, and the ball hit the pad, resulting in a leg bye.

**Paddle sweep:**

A batting shot played by sweeping the ball from outside the off stump towards the fine leg region.

Example: The batsman executed a well-timed paddle sweep, guiding the ball to the boundary for four runs.

**Partnership:**

The combination of two batsmen at the crease, working together to accumulate runs.

Example: The opening batsmen built a solid partnership, adding 100 runs for the first wicket.

**Penalty runs:**

Additional runs awarded to the batting team as a penalty for a breach of cricket laws by the fielding team.

Example: The fielding team was penalized with five penalty runs due to their excessive appealing.

### Perseverance:

The quality of showing determination and persistence in the face of challenges or setbacks.

Example: The bowler displayed great perseverance, bowling consistently in the right areas to create pressure on the batsmen.

### Pinch hitter:

A lower-order batsman sent in to bat aggressively and score quick runs in limited-overs cricket.

Example: The captain promoted the pinch hitter to accelerate the scoring rate in the middle overs.

### Pitch:

The central strip of the cricket field where the ball is bowled and the batsmen play their shots.

Example: The pitch was slow and offered some turn to the spinners, making it challenging for the batsmen.

**Play and miss:**

When a batsman attempts to play a shot at the ball but fails to make contact.

Example: The bowler beat the outside edge, and the batsman played and missed the ball.

**Powerplay:**

A designated period in limited-overs cricket where fielding restrictions are in place, allowing fewer fielders outside the inner circle.

Example: The batting team took full advantage of the powerplay, scoring quick runs in the first six overs.

**Pull shot:**

A batting shot played by pulling the ball from outside off stump towards the leg side.

Example:

The batsman executed a powerful pull shot, sending the ball soaring over the midwicket boundary for six runs.

**Pushed into the covers:**

A shot played by pushing the ball gently towards the fielders in the covers region.

Example: The batsman carefully pushed the ball into the covers, taking a quick single.

**Pacer:**

A fast bowler who bowls with significant speed and relies on pace to trouble the batsmen.

Example: The team included two pacers in their bowling attack to put pressure on the opposition batsmen.

**Powerplay:**

A designated period in limited-overs cricket where fielding restrictions are in place, allowing fewer fielders outside the inner circle.

Example: The batting team took full advantage of the powerplay, scoring quick runs in the first six overs.

**Power hitter:**

A batsman known for their ability to hit the ball with great power and generate maximum runs.

Example: The team relied on their power hitter to score big sixes and provide quick runs in the death overs.

Chapter 17

Q

**Quick:**

Refers to fast bowlers or pace bowlers who generate significant speed and bounce off the pitch.

Example: The team's quick bowlers troubled the opposition batsmen with their pace and bounce.

**Quick single:**

A run scored by the batsmen by running swiftly between the wickets after playing a shot.

Example: The batsman played the ball into the gap and called for a quick single, completing it comfortably.

### Quaffle:

In the sport of Quidditch (a fictional game), the ball used by the Chasers to score goals.

Example: The Chaser skillfully passed the quaffle to a teammate, who scored a goal for their team.

### Quaich:

A ceremonial cup used in some cricket competitions or presentations.

Example: The winning team was presented with a quaich as a symbol of their victory.

Chapter 18

R

**Rain delay:**
A temporary suspension of play due to rain, typically until the weather conditions improve.

Example: The match experienced a rain delay, causing the players to leave the field and seek shelter.

**Regulation:**
Refers to the official rules and standards set by cricket governing bodies to ensure fair play.

Example: The players must adhere to the regulations regarding the size and weight of the cricket ball.

**Reverse swing:**

A phenomenon in which a cricket ball moves in the opposite direction to the conventional swing.

Example: The bowler used reverse swing to deceive the batsman and take an important wicket.

**Reverse sweep:**

A batting shot played by a right-handed batsman sweeping the ball from outside off stump to the leg side.

Example: The batsman executed a reverse sweep, sending the ball past the fielder at short fine leg for four runs.

**Rubber:**

A series of matches played between two cricket teams, typically consisting of multiple games.

Example: The teams engaged in an exciting rubber, with each match contributing to the overall series result.

**Run:**

A unit of scoring in cricket, awarded to the batting team when the batsmen successfully complete a run between the wickets.

Example: The batsman played a well-timed shot and completed a quick single, adding one run to the team's total.

### Run chase:

The act of attempting to achieve a target score set by the opposing team during an innings.

Example: The team had a challenging run chase ahead of them, requiring a high run rate to win the match.

### Run-out:

A method of dismissing a batsman where the fielding team dislodges the bails before the batsman completes a run.

Example: The fielder showed great agility and accuracy to effect a run-out by hitting the stumps directly.

**Run-rate:**

The average number of runs scored per over in an innings, used to assess a team's scoring rate.

Example: The team needed to increase their run-rate to set a challenging target for the opposition.

**Run-up:**

The approach taken by a bowler before delivering the ball, typically involving a series of steps.

Example: The fast bowler had a long and smooth run-up, generating significant pace in his deliveries.

### Runner:

A substitute player who runs between the wickets on behalf of an injured batsman.

Example: The injured batsman was unable to run, so a runner was appointed to take his place.

### Run-feast:

A match or innings characterized by a high number of runs being scored by both teams.

Example: The match turned into a run-feast as both teams piled on the runs, thrilling the spectators.

Chapter 19

S

**Sabotage:**
An illegal action taken by a player to intentionally damage the chances of their own team or the opposition.

Example: The player was caught attempting to sabotage the match by tampering with the ball.

**Safe hands:**
Refers to a fielder who is known for consistently taking catches without dropping them.

Example: The fielder positioned at slip is known for his safe hands and rarely lets a catch slip by.

**Sandshoe crusher:**

A delivery bowled by a fast bowler that hits the batsman's shoe or the lower part of the leg.

Example: The fast bowler unleashed a sandshoe crusher that rattled the batsman's stumps.

**Score:**

The total number of runs accumulated by a team or an individual batsman during an innings.

Example: The team managed to post a challenging score of 300 runs on the scoreboard.

**Scoreboard:**

A display board that shows the current score, wickets, overs, and other match-related information.

Example: The scoreboard indicated that the team was trailing by 50 runs with five wickets remaining.

Score sheet:

A document used to record the scores, dismissals, and other statistical details of a cricket match.

Example: The score sheet revealed that the batsman had scored a century in the previous match.

Score chart:

A graphical representation of the runs scored by a team or an individual over the course of an innings.

Example: The score chart depicted the batsman's gradual accumulation of runs throughout his innings.

Seam:

The raised stitching on the cricket ball that helps the bowler generate movement off the pitch.

Example: The bowler pitched the ball on the seam, causing it to deviate after hitting the ground.

**Second innings:**
The batting opportunity for a team after the opposition has completed their first innings.

Example: The team performed well in their second innings, successfully chasing down the target set by the opposition.

**Short leg:**
A fielding position close to the batsman on the leg side, typically behind square.

Example: The fielder stationed at short leg took a sharp catch off the batsman's pads.

**Silly mid-off:**

A fielding position near the batsman on the off side, positioned close to the pitch.

Example: The fielder at silly mid-off attempted to catch the ball as the batsman played a defensive shot.

**Six:**
A scoring shot in which the ball clears the boundary rope without bouncing, resulting in six runs.

Example: The batsman smashed the ball over the long-off boundary for a magnificent six.

**Spin bowling:**
A style of bowling in which the bowler imparts spin on the ball to generate movement through the air or off the pitch.

Example: The spinner deceived the batsman with a flighted delivery that spun sharply away from the bat.

### Stumped:

A method of dismissing a batsman when they step out of their crease and the wicketkeeper removes the bails.

Example: The wicketkeeper was quick to react and stumped the batsman as he attempted to play a big shot.

### Swing bowling:

A style of bowling in which the bowler generates lateral movement through the air, either inwards or outwards.

Example: The swing bowler produced late outswing, beating the batsman's edge and hitting the off stump.

**Square leg:**

A fielding position on the leg side, square to the batsman.

Example: The fielder at square leg stopped a powerful shot and saved runs for the team.

**Slogger:**

A batsman who predominantly relies on power hitting rather than technique.

Example: The slogger in the team attempted to hit every ball for a boundary, regardless of its line or length.

### Slog sweep:

A batting shot in which the batsman swings across the line to hit the ball from outside the off stump towards the leg side.

Example: The batsman executed a perfect slog sweep, sending the ball soaring over the square leg boundary.

### Slips:

Fielding positions behind the wicketkeeper, on the off side, usually in catching positions.

Example: The slips cordon took a brilliant diving catch to dismiss the batsman and break the partnership.

### Spin bowler:

A bowler who primarily bowls spin deliveries, using finger or wrist action to impart spin on the ball.

Example: The team relied on their spin bowlers to take wickets in the middle overs.

### Square cut:

A batting shot played with a horizontal bat, hitting the ball square of the wicket on the off side.

Example: The batsman executed a powerful square cut, sending the ball racing to the boundary.

### Super Over:

A tie-breaking method used in limited-overs matches to determine the winner in case of a tie.

Example: The match ended in a tie, and the teams proceeded to a thrilling Super Over to decide the winner.

**Sweeper:**
A fielder positioned in the deep, typically on the off side or the leg side, to stop or catch shots hit along the ground.

Example: The batsman played a lofted shot, but the sweeper in the deep made a diving catch to dismiss him.

**Swing:**
The lateral movement of the cricket ball in the air, caused by the bowler's action and the condition of the ball.

Example: The swing bowler generated late swing, making it difficult for the batsman to judge the line of the delivery.

**Switch hit:**

A batting shot in which the batsman changes their grip and stance to play a shot opposite to their original handedness.

Example: The batsman surprised the bowler with a switch hit, sending the ball sailing over the backward point boundary.

Chapter 20

T

**T20:**

Abbreviation for Twenty20, a shorter format of cricket where each team gets to bat for a maximum of 20 overs.

Example: The T20 match between the two rival teams drew a huge crowd at the stadium.

**Target:**

The number of runs a team needs to score to win a match.

Example: The team set a challenging target of 250 runs for the opposition.

### Tea:

A break taken during longer-format matches, usually in the afternoon, when players have refreshments.

Example: The players enjoyed a cup of tea during the tea break.

### Test match:

A Test match is the longest and most traditional format of cricket, played between two international teams over a period of five days. It is considered the pinnacle of the sport and often showcases the highest level of skill, strategy, and endurance. Test matches are played with a red ball and white clothing, and teams compete to score the highest number of runs and take the opposition's wickets. The result of a Test match can be a win, loss, or draw, and it provides a comprehensive assessment of a team's performance over an extended period.

Example: The Ashes series features five test matches between England and Australia.

Third umpire: An off-field umpire who reviews on-field decisions using technology and provides decisions for certain situations.

Example: The third umpire was called upon to review a close run-out decision.

**Throw:**

The action of the fielder releasing the ball back to the wicketkeeper or another fielder.

Example: The fielder's accurate throw hit the stumps, resulting in a run-out.

**Toss:**

The process by which the captains of the two teams determine which team will bat or bowl first.

Example: The coin toss resulted in the home team winning and choosing to bat first.

**Trademark shot:**

A batting shot that a particular player is well known for and frequently executes.

Example: The batsman played his trademark shot, a powerful cover drive, for a boundary.

**Track:**

The condition and nature of the pitch on which the cricket match is being played.

Example: The spinners were able to exploit the turning track and take wickets.

**Turn:**
The amount of spin a bowler is able to generate with their delivery on a given pitch.

Example: The ball gripped the surface and turned sharply after pitching.

**Two-paced:**
Referring to a pitch that has uneven bounce or variable pace, making it challenging for the batsmen.

Example: The bowlers exploited the two-paced nature of the pitch to trouble the opposition batsmen.

Chapter 21

U

**Umpire:**

The officials responsible for ensuring the rules of the game are followed and making decisions on the field.

Example: The umpire raised his finger to signal the batsman out.

**Underarm bowling:**

A style of bowling in which the bowler releases the ball with an underarm action.

Example: Underarm bowling was commonly used in the early days of cricket.

**Unbelievable:**

Used to describe an extraordinary or remarkable cricketing performance.

Example: The batsman's century in the final over was simply unbelievable.

**Unplayable delivery:**

A delivery that is extremely difficult for the batsman to play or defend.

Example: The bowler bowled an unplayable delivery that swung late and took the edge of the bat.

**Unorthodox shot:**

A batting shot that is unconventional or not commonly seen.

Example: The batsman played an unorthodox reverse sweep to the fast bowler.

**Unpredictable bounce:**

Referring to the irregular or inconsistent bounce of the ball off the pitch.

Example: The pitch had unpredictable bounce, making it challenging for the batsmen.

**Upright seam:**

Referring to the position of the seam on the cricket ball, standing vertically.

Example: The bowler maintained an upright seam while delivering the swinging ball.

**Uppercut:**

A batting shot played with an upward swing of the bat, usually to hit the ball over the slips.

Example: The batsman played a powerful uppercut for a six over the third man boundary.

**Use of the feet:**

Referring to the batsman's technique of moving forward or backward to meet the ball.

Example: The batsman showed great use of the feet by stepping out and hitting the ball down the ground.

**U-Turn:**

Referring to the situation where a team's performance dramatically changes during a match or series.

Example: The team made a U-turn in the second innings and went on to win the match.

Chapter 22

V

**Victory:**

Referring to the successful outcome or win in a cricket match.

Example: The team celebrated their victory after chasing down the target.

**Video umpire:**

An off-field umpire who reviews on-field decisions using video replays and provides decisions for certain situations.

Example: The video umpire overturned the on-field decision after reviewing the close catch.

**Vinegar stroke:**

A term used to describe a batsman's aggressive shot or swing.

Example: The batsman played a powerful vinegar stroke and hit the ball out of the park.

**Volleys:**

Referring to the shots played by a batsman to deliveries pitched up by the bowler.

Example: The batsman confidently played a series of volleys for boundaries.

**Vulnerable:**

Referring to a team or player's susceptibility to getting dismissed or conceding runs.

Example: The bowler exploited the batsman's vulnerable off-stump and took regular wickets.

**Vulture:**

A term used to describe a fielder who takes catches or wickets at crucial moments.

Example: The fielder proved to be a vulture by taking a diving catch to dismiss the set batsman.

**Vulture mode:**

Referring to a bowler's aggressive approach in picking up wickets in quick succession.

Example: The bowler switched to vulture mode and took three wickets in an over.

# Chapter 23

## W

**Wagon wheel:**

A visual representation of a batsman's scoring shots on a cricket field, resembling the spokes of a wagon wheel.

Example: The batsman's wagon wheel showed a majority of his runs coming through the off-side.

**Walk:**

Referring to a batsman voluntarily leaving the field without being dismissed, often due to a gesture of sportsmanship.

Example: The batsman, realizing he had nicked the ball, decided to walk without waiting for the umpire's decision.

**Wicket:**

Refers to both the set of stumps and the playing surface between them. It is also used to describe the dismissal of a batsman.

Example: The bowler knocked the wicket and the batsman was out.

**Wicketkeeper:**

The player in the fielding team who stands behind the stumps and is responsible for catching the ball and affecting run-outs.

Example: The wicketkeeper took a brilliant diving catch to dismiss the batsman.

**Wide:**

A delivery that is deemed too wide of the batsman's reach and is called by the umpire. It adds an extra run to the batting team's score.

Example: The bowler's delivery was too wide, and the umpire signaled a wide.

Chapter 24

X

### X-factor:

Referring to a player or element in the game that possesses a unique or unpredictable quality, often capable of influencing the outcome of a match.

Example: The all-rounder's ability to take wickets and score quick runs adds an X-factor to the team's performance.

### Xpress:

Slang term used to describe a fast bowler with exceptional pace.

Example: The young bowler made an immediate impact with his xpress pace, regularly clocking speeds over 90 mph.

Chapter 25

Y

**Yorker:**

A type of delivery bowled by a fast bowler that lands near the batsman's feet, making it difficult to play an attacking shot.

Example: The bowler executed a perfect yorker, which crashed into the stumps.

**Yorker specialist:**

A bowler known for his expertise in bowling yorkers consistently and effectively.

Example: The team relied on their yorker specialist to deliver crucial wickets in the death overs.

### Yips:

A term used to describe a sudden loss of control or accuracy experienced by a bowler, often resulting in erratic deliveries.

Example: The bowler struggled with the yips, repeatedly bowling wide of the target.

### Yorker length:

The ideal length for a yorker delivery, which is aimed at the base of the stumps.

Example: The bowler adjusted his length and consistently bowled in the yorker zone.

## Chapter 26

## Z

### Zooter:

A term used to describe a type of delivery bowled by a spin bowler that skids through low and straight, often surprising the batsman.

Example: The spinner bowled a zooter, and the batsman misjudged the bounce, resulting in a bowled dismissal.

### Zing bails:

Specially designed bails that contain LED lights and are used in limited-overs cricket. They light up when the stumps are disturbed, providing a visually appealing effect.

Example: The bowler hit the stumps, and the zing bails lit up to indicate a dismissal.